The
DNA
of the
English
Language

JONATHAN
DUNNE

Published in 2007 by
SMALL STATIONS PRESS
1-A Jose De San Martin Street, 1111 Sofia, Bulgaria
You can order books and contact the publisher at
www.smallstations.com

Text and cover photographs copyright © Jonathan Dunne 2007
Design copyright © Yana Levieva 2007
Bible quotations contained herein are from the New Revised Standard Version, Anglicized Edition, copyright © The Division of Christian Education of the National Council of the Churches of Christ in the United States of America 1989, 1995
Cover photographs are of Eleshnitsa Monastery, near Sofia

Printed in Bulgaria by Bulvest
ISBN 978-954-384-001-4
A catalogue record for this book is available from the British Library

All rights reserved

The
DNA
of the
English
Language

JONATHAN
DUNNE

I SMALL STATIONS PRESS **I**
London & Sofia

for *Tsveta - sweet water, west east...*

16

You have to be able to hear the last note before you play the first.

Daniel Barenboim, end of the 2006 Reith Lectures

Balance is the embryo of wings.

Tsvetanka Elenkova, in conversation

8

O

The English alphabet contains 26 letters. Most of these letters on their own are not enough to form a word. Only a few vowels – *a*, *I* and *o* – can do that. The others need at least another letter. Words carry meaning. Put into a sentence, they communicate what we want to say. Adjectives are linked with nouns and preceded by an article: *a beautiful day, the young man*. Nouns or pronouns, which stand in for nouns, become the subject or object of verbs: *We _had_ a beautiful day*. Verbs may be qualified by an adverb: *The young man spoke _slowly_*. Prepositions precede a noun: *He was _in_ the room*. Conjunctions connect two sentences or parts thereof: *The young man spoke slowly _and_ quietly. He was in the room _but_ I didn't see him*.

By their connection and relation, to give the *Oxford English Dictionary*'s definition of *syntax*, words convey meaning. They are at our disposal, and we use them sometimes cautiously, sometimes carelessly. We (and our listeners or readers) may set great or little or no store by them. Spoken, they are carried off by the wind and, like our past, seem irretrievable. On paper, they acquire permanence and become legally binding. Much of our tradition, however, is transmitted orally. We may remember and have been influenced by words long since forgotten by the person who spoke them. And if the light of an extinct star is now reaching the earth, perhaps the spoken word, like our past, is not altogether lost and resonates still in another part.

Let us take a closer look at the act of speech and the letters used to represent the sounds we make when we articulate a word. We start with breath. From the moment we first scream as a baby, breath forms part of our vocabulary. What makes the scream so effective, however, is the addition of voice, which forms a vowel. A scream is represented *Aaaah!* or *Ooooh!* The letter that represents breath is the final **h**, perhaps the most important letter since it represents the basis of all speech, but silent in some languages and dropped colloquially.

Breath on its own does not form a word, it requires a vowel. If breath is wind, vowels are water. Hold a vowel for long enough, and water will collect in your mouth. This combination of breath and a vowel, wind and water, is all around us. We talk about the air's humidity, which becomes visible as mist, steam or rain. Bubbles of air form in water in a glass or kettle. The player of a wind instrument constantly has to release water through a valve. Plants to grow need wind and water, carbon dioxide from the air and hydrogen from the water, thus releasing oxygen from the water to replenish the earth's atmosphere.

As air passes through the windpipe and voice is added to it, vowels are produced in the mouth in the following order: **u**, **o**, **a**, **e**, **i**. The vowels **u** and **o** are back vowels, **a** is more or less central, **e** and **i** are front vowels; **u** and **i** are pronounced high in the mouth, **o** and **e** in the middle and **a** low. The vowels in this order form a u-shape, descending from **u** through **o** to **a** and ascending again through **e** to **i** at the front of the mouth.

Since **h** or breath alone does not make a word and it requires a vowel, the first word to be produced in the mouth as we breathe out and vibrate our vocal cords is *hu*. *Hu* represents the sound produced as wind and water combine for the first time. You can't get to a vowel sound without first breathing out, which makes *hu* the primal word. Search in the *OED*, and you will find that *hu* is Sanskrit for *invoke the gods* and the root-word for *God*. So the primal word, the first to form in the mouth as we breathe out and add voice, is the word from which *God* derives.

After **h** and the vowels, there are the semi-vowels: **j**, **y** and **w**. These are halfway between vowels and consonants, **j/y** corresponding roughly to the vowel **i** and **w** to **u**.

Then come the consonants. If **h** is breath and vowels are water, consonants are flesh. They are formed by obstructing breath with flesh – the lips or tongue – with or without the addition of voice. In the study of speech sounds known as phonetics, consonants are divided into 7 pairs:

b-p   d-t   f-v   g-k   l-r   m-n   s-z

These pairs are central to an understanding of how the English language works. Most of the consonants are voiced (you can test this by holding your throat as you pronounce them); only **p**, **t**, **f**, **k** and **s** are pronounced without voice and so voiceless.

While **b** is paired with **p** and **f** with **v**, there is also a strong connection between **b** and **v** (and **w**). We see this in languages such as modern Greek (**b** is pronounced **v**), Spanish (**v** is pronounced **b**), Latin (**v** is pronounced **w**) and German (**w** is pronounced **v**). So, in addition to the pairs **b-p** and **f-v**, we can make a further connection: **b-v-w**. The combinations **f-v** and **b-v-w** enable me, through **v**, to connect **f** with **b/w**.

Of the 26 letters in the alphabet (**h**, 5 vowels, 3 semi-vowels and 14 consonants), that leaves only 3. These are also consonants and are, in effect, redundant since they represent sounds already covered: **c** represents **k** or **s** (think of a word like *cancer*), **q** represents **k**, and **x** represents **ks**. This redundancy, however, brings one advantage since it enables me to connect **c** with either **k** or **s** (and so with **g** or **z**).

So speech sounds are a combination of breath and water (vowels) and/or flesh (consonants). To pronounce a voiced consonant such as **b**, I must use all three: breath, voice and my lips. To pronounce a voiceless consonant such as **p**, I need only breath and flesh (my lips), without voice. Breath, water and flesh are the three elements that go to make up speech.

Breath, water and flesh are also the three ingredients of creation. We read at the start of Genesis, 'In the beginning when God created the heavens and the earth, the earth was a formless void and darkness covered the face of the deep, while a wind from God swept over the face of the waters. Then God said, "Let there be light;" and there was light.'

A *wind* from God swept over the face of the *waters*. This enabled a word to come about, so that God *said*. Over the course of six days, related in chapter 1 of Genesis, God created the heavens and the earth through the word, by speaking (this is confirmed by the start of John's Gospel).

Later, in chapter 2 of Genesis, we read, 'But a stream would rise from the earth, and water the whole face of the ground – then the Lord God formed man from the dust of the ground, and breathed into his nostrils the breath of life; and the man became a living being.' Here, in the creation of man, we see a combination of the three elements breath, water and *the dust of the ground*, namely flesh.

So the act of speech mirrors the act of creation. In this book, I would like to suggest that as DNA carries genetic information, so language, in particular the English language, carries information about the origins and purpose of human life. This is a theory that will be presented less by rational, coherent argument than by the words themselves.

Etymology is the science that traces the history of a word, its formation and development. According to the *OED*, the English word *human* derives from the Latin *humanus*, relating to *homo*, man. But *human* is also a combination of *hu* – the root-word for *God* – and *man*. *Hu* makes us *hu*man.

In this book, I would like to suggest that words such as *past* and *star*, *air* and *rain*, *mist* and *steam* – even *space* and *speak* – are connected in a way that is far from random. Given that languages take centuries to evolve, such connections cannot be the work of a single man or woman living in a single generation. Like the rest of creation, where every part needs or feeds another, they reflect the design and presence of the supreme, immortal being we call God.

The three elements of speech and creation are *breath*, *water* and *flesh*. These words have *father* in common.

They are linked together – and with *create* and *word* – not randomly, but by a clear set of rules that revolves around the seven phonetic pairs.

Over the course of six days, God created the heavens and the earth. For each day, we read in Genesis, 'And God said.' The English language confirms this: the *world* we inhabit is a combination of *word* and *lord*.

1

In the beginning God created the heavens and the earth, man and woman. This is the story of creation related in chapters 1 and 2 of Genesis. God gave the man and woman free will and placed them in a garden, the garden of Eden, where they were allowed to eat of every tree, but he warned them not to eat of the tree of the knowledge of good and evil, 'for in the day that you eat of it you shall die' (Genesis 2.17). God did not build a wall around the tree of knowledge, fit it with security cameras and lights, he simply warned us not to eat of the tree or we would die.

The man and the woman – Adam and Eve – chose to ignore God's warning. Tempted by the serpent, Eve ate the forbidden fruit and gave some to her husband. This is the story of the Fall related in chapter 3 of Genesis. Instead of listening to God, they listened to the I (erotically represented by the serpent) and were expelled from Eden. The rest of the Old Testament is about how God's chosen people, the Israelites, repeatedly ignored God's warnings, put in the mouths of prophets, followed their own devices, got into trouble (defeat in battle or exile), repented, received God's mercy only to fall again after a period of prosperity. We still live in the era of the I, a world of conflicting egos: think of a traffic jam, for example.

Before making him the father of many nations, in Genesis 22, God tested Abraham to see if he would sacrifice his only son, Isaac, at God's command. In anticipation of the road to Calvary, when Jesus had to carry the Cross on which he would be crucified, Abraham even laid the wood of the burnt-offering on his son. God, however, did not allow Abraham to sacrifice his son and provided a ram instead. In the New Testament, God sent his only-begotten son, Jesus Christ, into the world to atone for our sins. Unlike Isaac, Christ was sacrificed. There is no overestimating the majesty, and humbleness, of this act. Christ, who is God, became human to show us how to turn away from following our own devices, from following the I, as a result of which we will die, and how to turn to God and live.

This progression from creation (A) to the Fall (I) to redemption (O) is documented by the English language. In Exodus 3.13, Moses asks God who he is to say has sent him to the Israelites. God replies, 'I AM WHO I AM.' In the creation, *hu* made us *hu*man, *am* created *an* (remember the phonetic pair **m-n**). *An* is the indefinite article, the one we use for countable nouns, nouns that have a plural, which is to say that *am* created *a man*.

The *man* was given a *name*, *Adam* (very close to *made*), and he in turn named all the creatures God brought to him. What is in a *name*? Quite a lot. A *name* does *mean* something. A *rose* by any other name would not spell *eros* and *sore* with the letters rearranged.

In the *garden of Eden*, the newly created man and woman were in *danger of need*! Instead of saying *amen* to God's warning not to eat of the tree of knowledge, they introduced *I* into the language, took some of the forbidden fruit and said *mine*. Already we have progressed from A to I. We should say *am* with reference to God, but already we have started to say *I'm*.

Can is the most wonderful verb. Using the phonetic pair **m-n**, we can turn *can* into *make* (by adding a final **e**). This is what God did during the creation: he made the heavens and the earth, he brought order out of chaos. This is what we are called to do during our lives: to make our dreams come true, to turn the chaos of illusion into the order of reality, and for this we need faith, the faith to move mountains, not in one dramatic leap, but slowly, patiently, the way rivers sculpt stone.

In Genesis 4, Eve bore Adam two sons, Cain and Abel. *Abel* was *able*, but didn't do it. In the name *Cain*, *can* has already been corrupted by *I*. Cain could, and he murdered his brother Abel, shedding the first blood on the ground. In Genesis 11, after the Flood, we read how 'the whole earth had one language and the same words' and the people set about building the Tower of Babel. Aware of what they might achieve (compare the expulsion from Eden in Genesis 3.22), the Lord came down and confused their language, scattering the people abroad over the face of all the earth. This was the beginning of foreign languages and the need for translation, a discipline we ignore at our peril since we are all required, in one way or another, to translate, to find meaning. *Babel* is connected with *apple* by the phonetic pair **b-p**. I can't help also seeing a connection between *Abel*, *Babel* and *Bible*, the Word of God delivered to the world of I and which promises *life*, most usually in translation.

There is a remarkable similarity between the words *evil* and *devil*, though they're not connected etymologically. According to the *Oxford English Dictionary*, *evil* derives from the Gothic *ubils*, *devil* from the Greek *diabolos*. It is as if, over successive generations, their meaning has brought them close. We can compare *God* and *good*. Again they're not connected etymologically, *God* deriving from the Sanskrit *hu* and *good* from the Gothic *gops*. But *God* is *good* and the *devil* is *evil*. It's normal that language should reflect this.

The reverse of *evil* is *live*. The reverse of *devil* is *lived*. The letters of *death* rearranged spell another past tense: *hated*. When we are born, a *veil* falls over our eyes, such that we think we see. We commit *vile* acts and do not realize that our *sin* is *seen*.

We read about this in the story of the man born blind in John, chapter 9. As Jesus passes by, his disciples ask him who has sinned, this man or his parents, that he was born blind. Jesus replies that the man was born blind so that God's works might be revealed in him. He spits on the ground, makes mud with the saliva and spreads the mud on the man's eyes, sending him to wash in the pool of Siloam (which means *sent*). The reverse of *eyes* is *see*, of *wash* is *saw*. It is no coincidence, then, that the man comes back able to see. The man, who was created out of mud, must wash the mud from his eyes in order to see.

No one credits the miracle, the man himself is perplexed, but one thing he sees clearly: that whereas before he was blind, now he can see by the action of the man named Jesus. The Pharisees drive him out of the synagogue for suggesting that Jesus is from God. Jesus finds him, and the man believes.

Each one of us is the man born blind. We are born blind into this world. The words *born* and *blind* are even connected by the phonetic pair **l-r** (with addition of **d**). But, as Jesus warns the Pharisees at the end of this story, it is not if we are blind that we have sin. Our sin remains when we think we see.

Jesus refers to this in the parable of the sower: 'The reason I speak to them in parables is that "seeing they do not perceive, and hearing they do not listen, nor do they understand"' (Matthew 13.13). The world is full of people who look but do not perceive, who listen but do not understand. They see only what is around them, hear only fragments of words and not the Word itself, forgetting that silence is half of language (the white space on this page) and to *listen* we have to be *silent*.

We are all like that until we realize our *need*, fall on our *knees* and *seek* healing. *Seek* and you will *see* (or as the translation of Matthew 7.7 puts it, 'Search and you will find'). *Hear* and *heal* are connected by the phonetic pair **l-r**. As the reverse of *eyes* is *see*, so *ear* and *hear* are connected by the addition of **h** (though their etymological roots are different in the *OED*).

Language is telling us that, to be healed, we need to hear the Word of God, who is Christ, the second person of the Trinity. This is why, at the end of the parable of the sower, Christ cries, 'Let anyone with ears to hear listen!' In the parable of the sower, a sower sows seed. Some seeds fall on the path and are eaten by the birds; some fall on rocky ground and do not have enough soil; others fall among the thorns and are choked. Others, however, fall on good soil and bring forth grain (how similar is *grain* to *rain*!).

The *earth* Christ plants a seed in is our *heart*. *Seed* and *heart* are *see* and *hear* with the addition of the phonetic pair **d-t**. The seed grows in the earth of our heart if we have eyes to see and ears to hear.

Christ was crucified on the Cross that the veil over our eyes might be torn in two, as we read in Mark 15.38: 'And the curtain of the temple was torn in two, from top to bottom.' There is a paradox here. After the Fall, Adam and Eve were ashamed of their nakedness. Being clothed, it was as if they were naked (and naked before the Fall, as if they were clothed). So we, having a veil over our eyes, think that we see. Only when the veil separating us from the divine – as the altar curtain in Orthodox churches separates the nave from the sanctuary – is torn, as happened at the Crucifixion, do we become blinded as if by a bright light (like Saul on the road to Damascus) and seek to be healed. We are like creatures that live in the earth, which do not realize they're blind until they emerge into the open.

Through his Crucifixion, arms stretched wide, belly exposed, Christ teaches us to lay down our life in order to find it. In Matthew 10.39, he tells the twelve apostles, 'Those who find their life will lose it, and those who lose their life for my sake will find it.'

It is the I that has to go, the I that recoiled from God's warning not to eat of the tree of the knowledge of good and evil, or else we would die. God was right. We do die. Or, to be more accurate, *I die*.

One of the things we do in educating our children

is teach them to count up from 1. Once you start counting, there's no knowing where you'll end up, and this is the dilemma our world finds itself in. Once you start counting in a line, where do you stop? House prices, executive salaries, energy consumption are all examples of this.

The answer is to count down from 1 to 0, from I to O or God. God is much nearer than we think. He is right behind us. Some would say that God is nowhere to be seen. Looked at in another way, *nowhere* is *now here*.

By counting down from I to O, we do not turn *live* into its reverse, *evil*, but into *love*. We do not *sin*, we become a *son*. We do not say *I'm*, we say *om*. It was for this that *Christ* went to the *Cross*. Even he was prepared to count down, to lose his life for our sake. So we complete the progression from A to I to O.

Christ asks in return that we lose our life for his sake. He tells us, 'Those who find their life will lose it, and those who lose their life for my sake will find it.' Manifestly we cannot keep the life we've got. This world full of walking Is must die. But how can we possibly lose our life for his sake and find it? Where's the sense in that?

It is another paradox of Christianity that when we draw a line through the I, we form two symbols: a Cross and a plus-sign. By following Christ, by walking the way of the Cross, which involves putting down the I (symbolized by the Cross) and is sometimes a painful experience, we discover who we really are. We find our life, our real life, which does not die. Death is like a veil. When we die, we tear it in two, as Christ did, and see the divine. We begin to live the eternal life, however, here on earth. This is why during Orthodox services the altar curtain is opened from time to time, allowing us to glimpse what lies beyond.

By turning to Christ, we *reclaim* what is ours: eternal life. And this – not flashing lights or unlikely healings – is the meaning of *miracle*.

| 2 |

So far we have seen connections between words with the same letters in the same order (*human - hu man, nowhere - now here*) and with the same letters rearranged (*earth - heart, listen - silent*). We have seen connections between words with the vowels changed (*God - good, sin - seen*). We have seen connections where consonants are changed following the phonetic pairs (*heal - hear, am - an*) and where letters are added (*man - name, air - rain - grain*).

I would like to take a closer look at connections between words made by changing the vowels. *Vowel* is connected with *flow* by the phonetic pair **f-v** (with addition of **e**). Vowels are water, they are fluid. Languages such as Arabic and Hebrew do not even write them down. So it is easy to make connections between words by changing the vowels. A vowel may be doubled (*God - good*) or lengthened (*sin - seen, mist - steam*). Very often an **e** is added, especially in final position (*can - make*). By far the most common correspondences are **a-e** (*bread - breed*) and **e-i** (*priest - spirit*), involving the last three vowels pronounced in the mouth. Also frequent are **a-o** (*road - door*), **e-o** (*enemy - money*) and combinations with **u** (*start - trust, soil - soul*). Then there is the progression from A to I to O: *am - I'm - om*.

So we can reverse the word *earth* and, by applying the pair **a-e**, find the number *three* (and also *ether*). Why should the number three be relevant to the planet Earth? Apart from the obvious fact that there are three persons in the Trinity, I can find two reasons. First, the *earth* – together with words with which it is connected: *tree, seed* and *sea* – was created on day *three*, as we read in Genesis 1.9-13. It is remarkable that the four things God created on the third day – the *earth*, every kind of fruit *tree*, plants yielding *seed* and the *sea* – are all themselves connected (by the pair **a-e**, the phonetic pair **d-t** and the alphabetical pair **r-s**).

The second reason is that, of the major planets orbiting the Sun, in order of increasing distance from the Sun, *Earth* is again number *three*. The order of planets is: Mercury, Venus, Earth, Mars, Jupiter, Saturn, Uranus, Neptune and, until recently, Pluto. We may note that we live on Earth, between love and war (the Roman gods Venus and Mars), and that heading in the direction of love takes us through the sky (the airborne messenger Mercury) to the Sun, while heading in the direction of war takes us under the sea (Neptune) to Pluto, god of the underworld. Church Fathers relate that, after their death, the souls of the righteous are carried through the sky by angels, while the souls of the damned are plunged by demons down into the earth (how close are *damn* and *demon*!). In our life on earth, we face a stark choice between making love or war – turning *live* into *love* or *evil* – and this choice derives from Adam and Eve eating of the tree of the knowledge of good and evil.

The earth Christ plants a seed in is our heart. As I

must die in order to come to new life – and *die* is simply *I* with the addition of **d** and **e**; to die is literally to shed the I – so a *seed dies* in the earth and gives birth to a root and shoot. The *root* and *shoot* resemble a *foot* and *tooth*, and are themselves connected by the alphabetical pair **r-s** (with addition of **h**). While a *root* below ground divides into *two*, the *tree* above ground divides into *three* and bears *fruit*. This shedding of the I, the outer husk, that gives birth to the life inside (the seed in the heart) is confirmed in John 12.24, when Christ says to Andrew and Philip and the crowd standing nearby, 'Very truly, I tell you, unless a grain of wheat falls into the earth and dies, it remains just a single grain; but if it dies, it bears much fruit.' This again is the meaning of laying down our life in order to save it, and is confirmed by language.

As *earth* and *heart* are connected, so *soil* and *soul* are connected by the pair of close vowels **i-u**. Soil and soul have more in common than they might seem to. According to the *Oxford English Dictionary*, soil is composed of 'fragmented rock particles with humus, water and air,' much like the human body, in the confines of which the soul exists like an aura. Soil can be treated, grows sick or exhausted, has a habit of creeping down a slope. It is resistive to electricity and, in soil marks, reveals its buried features. Soil covers the surface of the earth like a thin skin, as the soul surrounds the human body. And the meaning of the verb *soil* is what many of us do to our soul in this life: first, 'defile or pollute it with sin' at a time when we think we see, only to realize our blindness (and need) and seek to be 'absolved from sin.' To 'defile or pollute with sin' and 'absolve from sin' are the first two definitions given for the verb *soil* in the *OED*, which is curious since they appear to have the opposite meaning. This, however, is the message of Christianity: we are forgiven for our sins as soon as or even before we commit them, so long as we repent and seek that forgiveness. Language again confirms this: in the *crime* itself, there is *mercy*. And we find this double meaning in the reverse of *soul*, which is *loose*. In the first sense, we are 'promiscuous, dissolute, immoral;' in the second, 'free or released from bonds, fetters' (*fetter* with the phonetic pair **d-t** becomes *freed*). The danger for our *soul* is that somebody *sold*, *lost* or *stole* it.

If we apply the pair **a-e**, the reverse of *faith* is *thief*. The devil is always disposed to steal our faith. *Devil* is connected not only with *evil* and *lived*, *lied*, *vied* and *died*, *delve* and *livid*, *defy*, *defile*, *wile*, *wield* and *idle*, but also with *yield* (some connections are made using pairs of letters that look alike, **v-y** being a good example).

The *devil* would have us *yield* to temptation, an easy way out, a release or relief from our pain or frustration, choice (despite being trumpeted by the free marketeers) often being our downfall. We all seek pain relief, but pain purifies us, it makes us more humble. It helps us to understand others and what causes them pain. It makes us more equal. Pain is the underside of love. Without pain, love is an empty sentiment. If it stays and endures pain, especially in opposition to the I's wishes, love takes us out of ourself and makes us superhuman (I am not an advocate of pain in itself, the right thing is to find a balance, something God usually does for us, once we repent and undergo treatment for our soul, by alternating joy and pain, by giving us resting-places, the point being that pain is temporary).

One of the noblest things I ever saw was a tree bearing the advertisement: 'I cut down trees.' Trees, like bedridden patients, are an example of what I mean by not yielding to temptation, the easy way out. Trees take whatever we throw at them in the form of pollution, concrete, even a chainsaw, and slowly but surely give back love in the form of fruit, shade, warmth and oxygen. They are a living example of what it is to love in the face of opposition. It might be argued that, being rooted to the spot, like bedridden patients, they have no choice but to stay put. That is my point. The availability of choice is often our downfall. *Stay* acts like a *yeast*, but it is all too easy to *stray* instead.

If we *stray*, if the devil manages to *steal* our faith, we become *stale* and are 'no longer good for anything,' as Christ says in the Sermon on the Mount: 'You are the salt of the earth; but if salt has lost its taste, how can its saltiness be restored? It is no longer good for anything, but is thrown out and trampled under foot' (Matthew 5.13).

Salt is pain, it gives *taste* and makes things *last*. If we run away from our pain, we become *stale*. Christ was nailed to the Cross, he couldn't move, but to say he had no choice would be fatuous. He suffered temptation not only at the beginning of his ministry, when after his baptism he was led by the Holy Spirit into the wilderness for forty days, but also the night before his Crucifixion in the garden of Gethsemane. He did not yield. Enduring pain – often at the hands of others, seemingly through no fault of our own – is perhaps the most bitter experience of being a Christian. We break out in a sweat. Both sweat and tears taste of salt. Using the alphabetical pair **r-s**, we can connect *tear* and *sweat* with *water*. Using the combinations **a-e-i**, **b-w** and **r-s**, however, we can turn *sweat* and *bitter* into *sweet*.

Salt can be bitter, it makes us last. But society, with the ethos of competition, teaches us to be first. I once heard a business leader state on the radio that Britain needs a more competitive spirit. This is nonsense. This ethos, however, is inculcated in us from the moment we attend school and start taking exams. I can only come first if you come second, in the same way as you can only be rich if I am poor. This is why *first* – which contains *fist* – brings *strife*. This is really why we have war in this world, because I want more and you've got it. But if we consider the possibility that we are all one body in Christ, competition no longer makes sense, because then we are competing not against the other, but against ourself, who is the other. In Mark 12.29-31, we read that the first two commandments are to love the Lord our God with all our heart and to love our neighbour as ourself. In 1 John 4.20, we read that we cannot love God without loving our brother or sister. Language again confirms this. There are languages in which the translation of *we love ourselves* and *we love each other* is exactly the same, the reflexive pronoun being used in both cases: for example, Spanish *nos amamos* and Bulgarian *obichame se*. The Greek word for *God* is *theos* (present in words like *theology*); using the pair **r-s**, we can connect *other* and God or *theos*. In the other, we find God, and this is confirmed in the judgement of the nations: 'I was hungry and you gave me food, I was thirsty and you gave me something to drink... just as you did it to one of the least of these who are members of my family, you did it to me' (see Matthew 25.31-46).

We must lose our life in order to find it. In Mark 10.31, Jesus tells his disciples another seemingly contradictory statement: 'Many who are first will be last, and the last will be first.' We can understand that those who are first in this world will be last in the world to come, while the poor in spirit will be first.

The letters of *salt* rearranged spell *last*, but *last* contains *lst*. We can rewrite the above statement: 'Many who are first will be last, and the last will be lst.' *First* and *thirst* are clearly related, and salt makes us thirst (it also makes us last). So we have a circle:

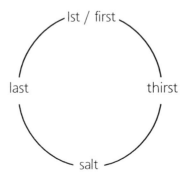

In John 4, Jesus meets a Samaritan woman near the city of Sychar. She has come to draw water at Jacob's well, and Jesus asks her for a drink. She is surprised that a Jew should ask her, a Samaritan, for a drink. Jesus replies, 'If you knew the gift of God and who it is that is saying to you, "Give me a drink," you would have asked him, and he would have given you living water.' The woman pithily remarks that Jesus has no bucket and the well is quite deep. Where does he get this living water? Jesus replies, 'Everyone who drinks of the water of the well will be thirsty again, but those who drink of the water that I will give them will never be thirsty. The water that I will give will become in them a spring of water gushing up to eternal life.'

The water of the well comes from without; the water of eternal life comes from within. We thirst in this world, but whatever the world can offer us will only satisfy our thirst for a time and we will have to return for more. The marketplace depends on this. It enslaves us. The water that Jesus offers us, however, feeds the seed in our heart and becomes 'a spring of water gushing up to eternal life,' so that we will 'never be thirsty.' It frees us.

In Mark 10.30, Jesus tells his disciples whoever has left family or home for Jesus' sake and for the sake of the Gospel will receive a hundredfold in this age 'with persecutions' – and in the age to come eternal life. The first are those who thirst, like all that is newborn. When we drink Jesus' 'living water,' we receive a hundredfold, but with the salt/pain of persecutions. We become last (this may have something to do with the cares and responsibilities of middle age). Salt gives taste, it preserves us, and those who last, who reach a calm old age, become first after their death and receive the gift of eternal life. So 'many who are first/thirst will be last – with salt – and those who last will be lst.' First and lst are not exactly the same, however, as the promised heaven is not a repeat of Eden (it couldn't be since *Eden* spells *need*). A second childhood is one with experience. Once we are lst, the connection between first and thirst is broken and we will 'never be thirsty' – we will never need – again.

Christianity is not a soft religion. Its message is stark and directly opposed to the world's message. The world teaches us to be first, Christ teaches us to be last (which is lst). The world teaches us to preserve our life (a blatantly futile task), Christ teaches us to give it up in order to keep it. The chief priests and scribes at the Crucifixion invite Jesus to come down from the Cross, so that they may 'see and believe' (Mark 15.32). The world says the same: 'See in order to believe.' Asking for a *sign*, however, is a *sin*. 'An evil and adulterous generation asks for a sign, but no sign will be given to it except the sign of the prophet Jonah. For just as Jonah was for three days and three nights in the belly of the sea monster, so for three days and three nights the Son of Man will be in the heart of the earth' (Matthew 12.39-40). This passage suggests that hell is in the centre of the earth, which we know to be fire (under the sea). Christ descends into hell after his Crucifixion to save the souls of Adam and Eve, the fallen man and woman, and rises on the third day. We must believe in order to see. The reverse of *believe* is *veiled* (as the sanctuary is veiled behind the altar curtain). We must *start* with *trust*, which is close to *thirst*.

In John 7.38, Jesus cries, 'Let anyone who is thirsty come to me, and let the one who believes in me drink. As the scripture has said, "Out of the believer's heart shall flow rivers of living water."' The Greek word translated as 'heart' is *belly*, and *Eve* resembles the Hebrew word for *living*. *Believe* contains not only *be* and *live* (to be found in *Bible*), but also *belly* and *Eve*. If we believe, out of our belly comes 'a spring of water gushing up to eternal life' and we are 'never thirsty.'

Christ on the Cross – the I deleted, which is also a plus-sign – teaches us that freedom is submission.

So often in this life we think that to be free means to be left to our own devices. We make a connection between *self* and *free*. This is the basis of most business; advertising appeals to the I. But freedom is not about having choices, as anyone puzzling in a supermarket aisle will tell you. The availability of choice has more to do with man's own insecurity and restlessness (need to keep busy). He doesn't trust a God to protect and provide for him, so he must do it for himself, using the fruits of the earth (he sells nothing of his own making), the source of which is unknown to him. He may not even believe in a God. Freedom is equated with movement, and pain is to be avoided at all costs. The worst case scenario is that of the tree or bedridden patient. And yet the ability to *flee* is not the same as to be *free*. The *tree*, rooted to the spot, may be more *free* than we are.

We only really have one choice in this life: to make love or war, to turn *live* into *love* or *evil*, to turn *life* into *fly* or *flee*. And it is curious that the only fly that can't, because it doesn't have wings, is a *flea*.

To be free is to walk through the eye of the needle (which I suspect is enormous if you catch it at the right angle, like the sun captured by leaves). Jesus looks at his disciples and says, 'For mortals it is impossible, but not for God; for God all things are possible' (Mark 10.27).

To be *free* is to walk the narrow path between *fear* (**a-e**) and *fire* (**e-i**). The fear is not the many unfounded fears inspired by the devil, it is Julian of Norwich's 'fear which makes us quickly flee from all that is not good and fall upon our Lord's breast like a child upon its mother's bosom' (*Revelations of Divine Love*, ch. 74, tr. Elizabeth Spearing). This *fear* is *safe* (**r-s**). The fire is the fire of purification. *Fire* is contained in *grief*. The clearest eyes I ever saw were of a widower at his wife's funeral. It is not a popular message. It is as if, to reach eternal life (the absence of time), we have to pass, like a grain of sand, through the narrow neck of an hourglass. It is not for the faint-hearted.

But we have a guide in Jesus Christ. Time is *change*. *Time* is our *chance* to *meet* Jesus and to acknowledge him as the Son of God. To believe in him. *Guide* removes us from *die*, *him* from *I'm*. Time, like a movable screen, is rolled away. And once we are *free*, it lasts for *ever* (**f-v**).

3

We have seen that connections between words can be made by using the same letters (in the same order or rearranged) and by changing the vowels. It is also possible to change the consonants, the flesh of language, and there are three ways of doing this: according to the seven phonetic pairs (and **b-v-w**); according to the alphabet; and according to the consonants' appearance.

We will look in more detail at the second and third ways in the following chapters, though we have already seen examples of both: for the alphabet, the most common pair is **r-s** (*fear - safe, other - theos*); for the consonants' appearance, normal correspondences are **b-d** (*believe - veiled*) and **v-y** (*devil - yield*).

By far the most frequent way of changing consonants, however, is by applying the seven phonetic pairs – **b-p**, **d-t**, **f-v**, **g-k**, **l-r**, **m-n**, **s-z** – and **b-v-w**. Some truly remarkable connections can be made by using the seven phonetic pairs. For example, we say that 'fire is life;' using the pair **l-r**, we see that *fire* is indeed *life* (and both are contained in *rifle*).

If we take away the letter **s**, we can connect *Christ* with both *child* (**d-t, l-r**) and *light* (**g-k, l-r**). That *Christ* might be *light* is confirmed by the connections *master - stream* and *lamb - lamp* (**b-p**). Christ is the *Lamb* of God who, without *blame* himself, takes our blame and applies *balm* to our wounds. On his entry into Jerusalem, people spread palms on the road. For a moment, they let go and unclenched their fists. *Palm* is connected with *psalm*, when we also open our hearts and lift them to God.

It was out of darkness that God created light in the beginning (Genesis 1.1-3). *Dark* is the reverse of *create* (**d-t**). It is *cold* (**l-r**). If we apply the three phonetic pairs

d-t, **g-k** and **l-r**, *dark* can be connected with *light* (addition of **h**). Seeming opposites are often connected in this way (compare *bitter - sweet*). *Fear* is *safe* – fear of evil – but *fear* is also *evil* (**f-v**, **l-r**) when we fail to have faith.

Turning to **b-v-w**, through **f-v**, we can connect *faith* with *way* and *wait*. As *faith* can grow *faint*, so *devout* can *doubt*. We connected *breath* with *create* (alphabetical pair **b-c**). *Breath* contains *earth* and is the *thread* (**b-d**) linking *birth* and *death* (**b-d**). *Birth* gives *third* in offspring: *birth* can be connected with *child* by using the pairs **d-t**, **l-r** and also **b-c**. It contains *rib* – woman was formed from man's rib, we read in Genesis 2.18-25 – which gives *RIP* (**b-p**). The reverse of *birth* is *tribe*, and it is intimately connected with *thrive* and *writhe*.

These connections alone ought to tell us that the English language is full of hidden roots, so-called coincidences, that go back to the very beginning and the story of creation related in Genesis. Through the combination **f-b/w**, *father* is connected with *breath* and *water* (addition of **h**). *Breath* is connected with *create*, *water* with *word* (**d-t**). Using **l-r** and also **s-t**, we can connect *father* and *flesh*. Through the combination **f-w**, we can connect *word* with both of them.

Christ is 'the Word made flesh' (John 1.14). It is not

that language gives us a connection to God, it is that language is God, but we throw words about without realizing this as we fail to see God's presence in every aspect of his creation. It is perverse in the extreme to deny the author of creation just because, through our own blindness, we cannot see him. 'I can't see him, therefore he doesn't exist.' This is the stance of the *Pharisee* (*far I see!*). We have splintered the Word into fragments of words just as we erect borders all over the earth – and in the sea – claiming that the land is ours. We make business out of the fruits of the earth, buying and selling property, bombarding each other with advertising messages (thereby laying claim even to the air), releasing and cutting off oil and gas. We attack each other with noise, something that Nature never does. And yet the God who watches over all this remains patient, waiting for each one of us to repent, to change our way of thinking, to acknowledge him. We get upset if someone steals an idea (and the idea isn't ours, it comes to us). Meanwhile Christ – the *guide* and *judge* – waits out of love! This is why those who say that humankind never learns are mistaken. In every generation, counted numbers repent and turn to Christ. As St Peter writes in his second letter, 'The Lord is not slow about his promise, as some think of slowness, but is patient with you, not wanting any to perish, but all to come to repentance' (2 Peter 3.9).

Christ is the Word, the second person of the Trinity, the Trinity like three butterflies criss-crossing and flying in a single direction. If God the Father is the eternal figure of O, Christ is O_2, the chemical formula for oxygen. We not only speak him, we breathe him. *Breath* – or the Holy Spirit, represented, as we saw, by the letter H – proceeds from the *Father* and combines with the Son (O_2) to make water: H_2O. And breath and water combine to make a word.

This combination of H and O_2 – hydrogen and oxygen – caused the Flood, a cry of anguish because of humankind's wickedness: 'And the Lord was sorry that he had made humankind on the earth, and it grieved him to his heart' (Genesis 6.6). *Word* and *flood* are connected (**l-r**, **f-w**). The reverse of *word* is *drown* (addition of **n**).

Using the pair **d-t**, we can see a remarkable similarity between *bread*, *breast* (addition of **s**) and *breath* (addition of **h**). They all contain *aer* (*air*) in reverse and are sources of nourishment: physical, maternal and spiritual. *Breast* is one of the most prolific words in terms of word connections. It contains *beast, sabre, stare, rest, east, seat, sate, bare, tear, stab, star, bra* and *sea* among others. It is connected through **b-p** with *priest* and *spirit*; through **b-v-f** with *starve* (which is in *harvest*) and *feast* (which contains *fast*). Through **l-r**, it is connected with *blest*, the epithet of the Virgin Mary; through **b-d**, with *drest*: before the Fall, Adam and Eve were unaware of their nakedness, they were as if clothed, an innocence still shared by primitive peoples and small children.

As breath and water combine to make a word, so bread and water combine in the Word. We consider *bread* and *water* the basic diet, and they are connected through **d-t** and **b-w**. We know, however, that if today we eat bread from the baker's and drink water from the tap, tomorrow we will again be hungry and thirsty. This is why Jesus offers the Samaritan woman 'living water,' so that she will 'never be thirsty.' Later, in John 6.35, Jesus calls himself 'the bread of life.' His are the spiritual bread and water that sustain for ever. We partake of this living bread and water when we open our hearts to receive God's Word. It is not a coincidence that *word* is connected with *sow* (**r-s**, addition of **d**). The Word is the seed Christ sows in the earth of our heart, the soil of our soul.

A more tangible form of this spiritual sustenance is found in the Lord's Supper, the Eucharist, when we eat Christ's body and drink his blood. Christ is the Word, so we open our hearts to receive his Word. Language again confirms this. In the Eucharist, the elements of bread and wine are consecrated by the Holy Spirit: a combination of *beer*, wine and spirit. Or again: *grain*, *grape* and *grace*. *Body* and *blood* are also connected, capital **I** and lower case **l** resembling each other (and **y** relating to **i**).

It is this spiritual food that Jesus refers to when, after fasting for forty days and nights, he is tempted to turn stones into loaves of bread. He answers the devil, 'It is written, "One does not live by bread alone, but by every word that comes from the mouth of God"' (Matthew 4.4). He gives a similar answer when his disciples find him after his conversation with the Samaritan woman and urge him to eat: 'I have food to eat that you do not know about' (John 4.32). And this may explain the link between *starve* and *harvest*, *fast* and *feast*. Physical food will arouse the taste buds and fill the stomach, but in the end it perishes. We need another food, 'the food that endures for eternal life, which the Son of Man will give you' (John 6.27).

In this, as in every way, Christ fulfils the Old Testament. He fasted for forty days and nights. The Flood lasted for forty days and nights. The Israelites spent forty years in the wilderness, receiving bread from heaven and water from the rock (see Exodus 16-17). The word *manna* (the term used by the Israelites to describe the bread from heaven, which appeared in the morning like frost on the ground and melted with the rising sun) derives from the Hebrew *man*, while the English *man* derives from the Gothic *manna*, and both are surely connected with *am* and *an*. The Israelites are freed from slavery in Egypt, but do not immediately reach the promised land. This is a metaphor for our conversion: once we turn to God and are freed from slavery to ourself, we still have a way to go – with plenty of complaining and dragging our heels! – before reaching eternal life.

We hunger and thirst in this world. We are peppered with holes right down to our pores, and I don't think we know what to do with them. *Hole* and *soul* are closely related. Ever since the Fall, we have been in need. We come out of what was hopefully a safe and loving childhood and face the task of finding our place in a world spinning through space. We are subject to sickness, uncertainty and a limited physical existence prior to death. Most of the world seems more interested in enjoying this life, or at least in getting by, and not worrying about the next (if it even exists). Everything we learn at school prepares us for human society – communicating, counting, finding out where we live, what we've done, etc. – and yet we're taught very little about how to love each other. Actually we're rather encouraged to indulge in some healthy competition, we're marked up or down and separated. Adults are just children who've grown up and lost their innocence and, if we're lucky, we spend the rest of our adult life, having been hurt, trying to recover that innocence, whereby we do not hurt (*innocent* means *not hurting*).

Our first response to the wide, open world is to take our 'freedom' (ability to do what we like, to move in any direction) and indulge our senses, often to excess. It is no coincidence that the reverse of *excess* is *sex*. We might eat/drink/smoke too much and sleep around. This is called 'having a good time.' But we have a good time at the expense of eternity. Soon (if we're lucky) the veil wears thin. We realize that the world is not our friend, it was just taking our money. We search for something more, something that will satisfy us a little longer, something that will fill not just our physical hole, but our spiritual need. We turn to God and say, 'Lord, have mercy.' Once we do this with sincerity in our heart, God answers us. It is an everlasting mercy that God is not a ruthless tyrant (like the devil) and that the *divine* actually wants us to *find* (**f-v**) him.

Lust turns us into a *slut*, who may be *lush*, but

eventually turns to *rust* as a *stud* turns to *dust*. We try turning *hole* into *whore* (**l-r**, addition of **w**) to fill our need, but it doesn't work.

It doesn't work until we discover love: both love for the other and that we are loved. *Love* provides the magic ingredient and makes us *whole* (**v-w**, addition of **h**).

Soul is connected not only with *hole*, but with *eros*. We find the other/*theos* and are no longer *sole* or alone. We enter his hole – one of the Hebrew names for God in the Old Testament is *Elohim*, which in reverse reads *my* or *I'm hole* – and are faithful to him.

That God is eros is confirmed by language. *Eros* is *zero* (**s-z**), the eternal figure of God, the first number we need to learn. And one of the strongest word connections: if we apply **l-r**, **v-w** and the alphabetical pair **d-e**, we see that *word* is *love*.

4

God is *nowhere* to be seen, he is *now here*, in the same way as we can move miles *apart* and yet we are still *a part*.

A teenage student of mine, Nadya, once wrote the motto, 'Kneel before no one!' It was an affirmation of personal identity, of standing out from the crowd, of resistance in the face of adversity. And yet the motto calls for complete submission. In affirming her own separate identity, she is advocating submission of that identity to another, losing her life in order to find it.

The word G O D is made up of 3 Os, which we could write O_3. God the Father would be O, God the Son O_2 and God the Holy Spirit O_3 again. And yet we are taught that God the Trinity is three in one, not zero. There is no contradiction here, however. The word O N E contains the numbers 0, 2 (on its side) and 3 (in reverse), not 1. ONE supports the theory that the Father is O, the Son O_2 and the Holy Spirit O_3: three in ONE.

The ancient Greeks at the oracle of Delphi referred to God as mēdĕn, which means *no one*. *One* is *no* reversed with the addition of final **e** (so common in word connections). God is *no one*. In chemistry, we do not add the subscript 1 (O_1), we simply write O.

God is 01. We see this combination of 0 and 1 everywhere in the world around us: in binary code, in our sexual organs, in an egg and seed, in a raindrop, in the stick figures of humans. 0 is the circumference of 1, 1 the profile of 0. Merge them together, and we have the earth spinning on its axis or the symbol *phi* (clearly related by addition of **h** to *pi*).

A book could be written just about the presence of 01 in the world around us. What we forget when counting from 1 is that 1 is only possible because of 0, as a word on the page needs the white space, as music starts with silence, as I am only possible because of O.

But we have a habit of putting I first and forgetting O. The Romans were praised for building long, straight roads (Is). For a time, we even believed the earth was flat, like I. We have spent most of creation drawing *line* after line and saying, 'This is *mine*!'

God gave us dominion over all things and said, 'Be fruitful and multiply!' (Genesis 1.28). The symbol for multiply is x: a kiss or a cross. But we have perverted this, erected the cross and made business: + − ÷. Instead of listening to *prophets*, we prefer to pay attention to *profits*.

We pervert the natural order. We would pervert God himself. If God is 01, humans are ten or 10. This is confirmed by the celestial hierarchy: in Christian theology, there are nine ranks of angelic beings from seraphim and cherubim to archangels and angels, which makes us number ten.

There were nine major planets, but we searched for a tenth. We count by tens. And as *three* was connected with *earth*, so is the number ten. The disciples were fishermen. Jesus calls them from their nets to 'fish for people' (Matthew 4.19). In this sense, we as fish have to be caught by the net's intersections, by the Word. But St Antony of Egypt has another image, that of the devil casting a net over the world, through which we as fish have to escape to reach salvation. We have to slip through the interstice.

In Seraphim Rose's book *The Soul after Death*, we read how souls after their death have to pass through various toll-houses in the sky, where they are accused by demons of wrongdoing in their life. If the balance of their good deeds is outweighed by their sins, the accompanying angels have to let go of them. This is the net I am talking about. It is not that we have to be perfect, rather that we need Christ, who takes our sins upon himself if we believe in him.

There are many word connections here. *Net* is the reverse of *ten*. Using the phonetic pair **d-t**, we can connect them with *need*, *den* and *end*. When Christ overturns the tables of the money-changers in the temple, he says to them, 'It is written, "My house shall be called a house of prayer;" but you are making it a den of robbers' (Matthew 21.13). They are connected by the phonetic pair **m-n** with *teem* and *time*: at the *end* of *time*, Christ will come again to judge the living and the dead.

In our life, we have to grow wings so that we can fly,

or perhaps simply we have to believe in them. We are surrounded on this glorious *planet* (containing *net/ten* and connected with *temple*) by examples of creatures that fly: birds. We have to grow fins so that we can swim like fish. In a sense, when we 'have a good time,' we are like fledglings, growing our feathers. But we cannot stay like fledglings in the *nest* (addition of **s**).

Fin is connected with *wing* by the pair **f-w** (addition of **g**). *Fly* is connected with *swim* by the alphabetical pair **l-m** (**f-w**, addition of **s**). *Air* is connected with *bird* by the alphabetical pair **a-b** (addition of **d**). *Aer* is connected with *sea* by the alphabetical pair **r-s**. Language is again trying to tell us something: perhaps that, when we swim, we already know how to fly. There are, after all, flying fish and birds like eiders or shearwaters that are good swimmers.

Man is naturally a *land* animal but, as a *plant* reaches to the light, so man must grow towards the light, who is Christ. David Attenborough in his astonishing nature programmes teaches us that life needs wetness and warmth. *Life* needs *light* and in the sea, where life began 3,000 (!) million years ago, life is abundant precisely where there is light.

Look at a depiction of Christ, or of a saint, and you will see a halo. I believe that the halo, this disc of light around the head, is not just what is termed in the *Oxford English Dictionary* 'an aura of glory,' it is the Sun (the Greek word for *sun* is *helios*). As hell was connected with the fire at the earth's core, so I would connect heaven with the Sun. We move in the direction of love (Venus), though of course we insist on sending probes in the other direction, to Mars. We move through the sky (the airborne messenger Mercury). And we come to heaven, where the Son is.

This is why it was vain to search for a tenth planet, because it already exists. Count down from *nine*, and you will come to *none*, a circle, the Sun (in a child's drawing, surrounded by rays, lines of light; *ray* is connected with *air*). But because we forget to count from 0, we thought the tenth planet was still out there, waiting to be discovered, and came across the dwarf planet 'strife' or Eris. We preferred to look into the outer reaches of space than accept the Sun, which is all around us, which never stops shining (at night, we turn away from it). *Light* is connected alphabetically with *might* and *night*, and then with *right* and *sight*.

We are told not to look at the Sun or we will be blinded! It seems we are terrified of learning that we cannot see, we are not the king, of opening our eyes in water! Perhaps this is the meaning of the obvious connection between *sea* and *see*. We are born out of water. We are baptized in water. Before we die, we become like a fish on dry land, gasping for breath. God created the sky by separating the waters from the waters – this is why we float in space – on the second day, after he created light (see Genesis 1.6-8).

If Christ is the Sun – we speak him (the Word), we breathe him (O_2), we drink him in water (H_2O) and we see by him – I believe that the MOON is a combination of Christ (O_2) and the Holy Spirit (O_3), which causes the *tide* and pulls us in when we *die*. The Son and the Holy Spirit combine in both water (which covers approximately 2/3 of the earth's surface) and the moon (which just happens to be 230,000 miles from the earth).

The *ego* is not *God* (*ego* is connected alphabetically with the words *foe* and *fog*). The *I* must *die* as the *self* must go the way of all *flesh*. It is *false* and a *slave*. But *slave* contains *law* and *save*.

On our *death*, we are in *debt* (**a-b**, addition of **h**). The demons claim us, but I am forgiven what I *owe* if I *obey* God's law to love him and to love my neighbour. I turn *self* into *serve* (**f-v, l-r**). The scrap of paper, *I.O.U.*, becomes an exclamation of joy: *I – O You!* This exclamation is itself contained in the word *you*. And through that recognition of the other we find ourself in *joy*: *I – O I!* We lose our life in order to save it in Christ. This is Christ's message in John 12.23-26 (quoted in part earlier): 'The hour has come for the Son of Man to be glorified. Very truly, I tell you, unless a grain of wheat falls into the earth and dies, it remains just a single grain; but if it dies, it bears much fruit. Those who love their life lose it, and those who hate their life in this world will keep it for eternal life. Whoever serves me must follow me, and where I am, there will my servant be also. Whoever serves me, the Father will honour.'

The whole of language cries out: *believe* and you will *receive* (**l-r**, **b-c**). Kneel before no one!

5

We have seen how consonants can be changed according to the phonetic pairs and the alphabet. Examples of the second kind of change are: **a-b** (*air - bird*), **b-c** (*believe - receive*), **d-e** (*word - love*), **k-l** (*walk - wall*), **l-m** (*land - man*), **p-r** (*past - star*), **r-s** (*aer - sea*) and **s-t** (*flesh - father*). Using **r-s**, we can now connect *hear* and *see*, *heart* and *seed* (**a-e**, **d-t**, with addition of **h**).

A third way of changing consonants is according to their appearance. In this way, a letter is reversed or upturned or continued. The letter **b** is reversed to **d** in *birth* - *third* and *breath* - *thread*. The letter **m** is upturned to **w**. *Mars* is the Roman god of *war* (addition of **s**). *Sweat* rises in *steam*. The *mind* can be fickle like the *wind*. It is a short step from *me* to *we*. Similarly the letter **n** is upturned to **u**. *Anger* causes us to *argue*. *Blind* can *build* (as *deaf* can *feed*). Occasionally a letter is rotated, as **d** to **p**. A *seed* has been known to *sleep* in the ground for hundreds of years before sprouting (addition of **l**).

Letters are continued. The letter **r** is continued to **n**, and **n** to **h**. **H** is pronounced **n** in the Cyrillic alphabet. We have to *work* in order to *know* (if we *work*, we *grow*). We can *pray* when we are in *pain* (and *pain* is linked to *pay* and *happy*). *Hair* falls like *rain*. If we have *hope*, we are *open*. The letter **v** is continued to **y** when the *devil* tempts us and we *yield*.

The naturalist David Attenborough is a poet because in his narrative he maintains a thread, seeing the similarity between different things. In the opening sequence of his nature programme *The Living Planet* (first broadcast in 1984), he makes a link between the earth and an eye. If you take a cross-section of the earth, it is true that the crust, mantle and core closely resemble the different parts (rim, colour and pupil) of an iris. God is the eye and he watches closely.

The *eye* is circular: O. The *I* is a straight line, and for a time we believed that the earth was flat, not round. We also believed that the earth was the centre of the universe. We made the earth to be like the I, which it is not.

In the garden of Eden, instead of saying *amen* to God's command not to eat of the tree of the knowledge of good and evil, Adam and Eve said *mine*. Eve took the forbidden fruit, ate some and gave it to her husband. There is surely a connection between *Eve* and *eye*.

We, however, are not the eye (I) of the world. When we subscribe to this view, we draw a line through the I (the symbol of the Cross). We count from I to O in *live* to *love*, *sin* to *son*, *nine* to *none*, and acknowledge the Sun as the centre of the universe.

And so we make the progression from A to I to O. This can be represented as: A † O. We saw, however, that deleting the I also makes a plus-sign: A + O. Using the reduced form of *and*, 'n', we can write this: A N O. When we take away the I, we actually make an addition: A N D.

We should not be surprised at the paradox. In Genesis

2.24, we read that 'a man leaves his father and his mother and clings to his wife, and they become one flesh.' The addition of a man and a woman (2) turns out to be a subtraction since 'they become one flesh' (1). The same thing happens when a woman gives birth. In order to multiply, she has to divide from her foetus.

The reverse of *and* is *DNA*, which is defined in the *Oxford English Dictionary* as 'a self-replicating material present in nearly all living organisms as the carrier of genetic information and the determiner of protein synthesis, usually occurring as a molecular double helix in which a phosphate group alternates with a deoxyribose sugar linked to a base.' Mother and father join to produce a child (an upturned triangle); out of their union comes offspring, a boy and a girl (a triangle). The two shapes superimposed pulsate like a kaleidoscope and give the Star of David. Three becomes five becomes eight, like an octave.

This union of a man and woman is a spiritual act, in which, like *nature*, we *return* to God (as music returns to silence). Our need is met through the other: our nakedness is clothed/filled. Our legs intertwined resemble the two strands of DNA, criss-crossing in a self-replicating 8. Our nimbuses merge in a heart shape, like an angel's wings.

I am interested in how the DNA strands are said to be 'linked to a base.' This recalls the act of translation, in which we carry meaning across an intervening space, from 'original' to translation, though the 'original' is no more original than the translation itself. There is a sense in which both already exist, and we just have to see or hear them. Both translate the reality we perceive – or receive – on to paper. Writing should be understood as a form of translation rather than the other way round.

We can view the translation process as a straight line, in which we work in isolation with the reality/text in front of us. A line – a wall or a tower – is structurally unsound. *Wall* is connected with *fall*, and walls and towers have a habit of coming down. Or we can acknowledge the source, the 'base,' work with the Spirit and form a triangle – a pyramid – which is structurally sound. By acknowledging the *third* point, we give *birth* to the line. We do the same when we go from I to O.

The waters have broken and begin to flow. As we cross now, our *bow – boat –* has something to play on. We no longer *play* as children, isolated in our own little world. We *pray* with reference to a third point and produce not just notes, but words with meaning. Like St *Christopher*, we carry the child *Christ over* the river. It is faith in the Christ-child that prevents us from drowning or being swept away.

This is man's destiny: to give birth to the I, to open his eyes, by producing a Cross, a circle or a triangle. The reverse of *cross* is *source*. We acknowledge the source and depart from the timeline of past, present and future. As we connected *time* with *end*, we can connect *time* with *begin* (**b-d-t**, **m-n**, addition of **g**). We recognize that there is a beginning and an end: A † O, or Alpha and Omega.

Omega is the last letter of the Greek alphabet, written Ω, ω. If we rewrite A N O, using the Greek letter, we have A N W, which gives *man*.

We are not the eye, God is the eye (I) of the world: A I O. If we rewrite this, we have A I W, which is the first strong indication in language that Jesus Christ is the Son of God. A I W gives *I AM*, the name God tells to Moses in Exodus 3.14. It also gives *way*. Christ was crucified on the Cross in order that we, who are dust, might have a *way* to return to God. Tsvetanka Elenkova, in her poem *Leonardo's Cross* (from her book *The Seventh Gesture*), points out the difference between the pagan figure of *The Vitruvian Man*, 'with legs outstretched,' poised to flee, and the figure of Christ on the Cross, with legs joined, poised to fly. Christ makes this connection between *I AM* and *way* when he says to

Thomas, 'I am the way, and the truth, and the life. No one comes to the Father except through me' (John 14.6).

We have seen the resemblance between capital **I** and lower case **I**. A I W gives *law*. In Matthew 5.17, Christ says that he has come 'not to abolish but to fulfil' the law. When in Mark 12.29-31 he commands us to love the Lord our God with all our heart and to love our neighbour as ourself, he is reiterating commandments given in the Old Testament (Deuteronomy 6.4-5 and Leviticus 19.18).

We, however, have a different perception of *law*, as in the Roman alphabet we do not count down from A to I to O, we count up: from A to I to Z (2). The *law* of man is not to love our neighbour. It is erected like a *wall*. Legal processes are time-consuming and expensive. Most of us see the law as something threatening, to be avoided. Man-made law protects private interests, the rights of the individual to own land, to conduct business, to lay claim. It punishes those who would take what belongs to another human being. But it is difficult to see how land, products of the land, even ideas, belong to anyone but the God who created them and gave them to us to name.

We proceed to draw lines and to say, 'Mine! Hands off!' We produce a legal document to prove it – again our reliance on what we think we see – which we ourselves have written. Daniel Barenboim in his 2006 Reith Lectures points out that we begin to hear in the second month of gestation while we do not see until we are born, and it is interesting to me that Christ spoke the Word. He himself, who is the Word, didn't write it down. He left that task to the translator Evangelists.

The *rule of law* is trumpeted as the only secure way to avoid conflict but, as so often in this world, the difficulties – such as conflict, starvation, unemployment – we set ourselves to solve are the consequences of our own actions. By drawing a line, we open ourselves to the *lure of war*. Without a line, there is nothing to fight over. *War* is connected with *law* by the phonetic pair **l-r**.

And the translator, hatched at Babel, works tirelessly like a spider to heal the rift, his threads occasionally broken, occasionally glinting in the sunlight. The translator, who doesn't believe in the line, who is willing to trespass the line, is forced out on to the line itself ('the Son of Man has nowhere to lay his head,' Matthew 8.20). Propertyless and practically without rights, he is forced to walk the narrow line, like a tightrope walker (another symbol of the Cross) suspended in mid-air, with only faith to hold on to. Peter, walking on the water, becomes afraid and begins to sink. Jesus catches him, saying to him, 'You of little faith, why did you doubt?' (Matthew 14.31).

In no man's land by now, the translator is entangled in the crossfire. He longs but stubbornly refuses to come down, because that would mean taking sides, accepting the existence of a line, border, barrier. He clings to his dream of the brown, barren, polluted land once again sprouting *grass* that covers the *scar*.

And he raises his arms to *laud* the *Lord* in a hymn of praise that again is represented by the Cross.

6

By adding letters and, where necessary, applying the rules for changing vowels and consonants, we can make strands of DNA out of the English language, which are sometimes very pretty indeed. Needless to say, two good starting-points are the indefinite article *a* and the subject pronoun *I*. Like a swiftlet making its nest out of beads of saliva or a silkworm adding globs of mucus to lasso its prey, we can incorporate letters to a word:

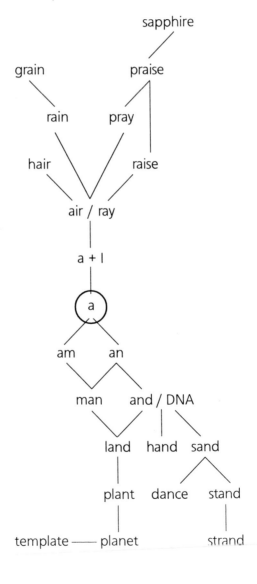

These patterns begin to look very like molecular structures (the link between chemistry and language is strong). A good example is *I*:

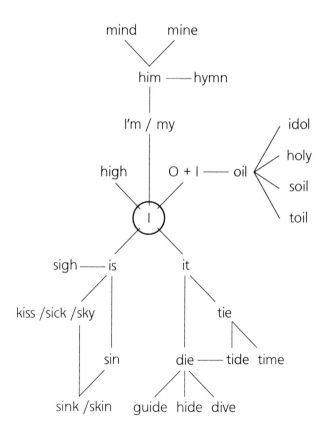

Letters are added to a word as in the formation of chemical compounds. We saw that H (Spirit) combines with O_2 (Son) in water (H_2O), and breath and water combine to make a word (who is Christ). Water is distributed by the Sun and wind, or Son and Spirit, its constituent elements. We saw that GOD and the Holy Spirit can be represented as O_3, which is the chemical formula for ozone, the layer that protects us from the fire (wrath) of the Sun (Son). The depletion of the ozone layer is due to emissions of carbon (C, atomic number 6, a number traditionally associated with the devil). These emissions are caused by our own wickedness, our lack of concern for the other – the devil enlists us, as it were (*wicked* and *devil* are connected by **v-w** and **k-l**) – which is what caused the Flood.

In our wickedness, we would pervert God, turning *God* into *ego*, OI (no one) into IO (ten) or *oil*. We fight over *oil* like spoilt children. We make of it an *idol*, a source of *toil*. When expelling the man from Eden, God said to him, 'Cursed is the ground because of you; in toil you shall eat of it all the days of your life' (Genesis 3.17). God put us to till the *soil*, a form of *oil* that is rarely talked about and without which we would go hungry. But there is another kind of oil, the one we pour on salads, the one we use to anoint children at their baptism. This *oil* is *holy*.

As we have turned away from God, so God would bring us back to himself by adding **h** and **g**. *I* gives *high*, *one* gives *home*, *die* gives *guide*, *I'm* and *mine* give *him*. A *host* is an army, it is also consecrated bread in the Eucharist and is connected with *ghost*, the Holy Spirit. The letters **h** and **g** follow and together spell the sixth letter of the alphabet, **f** (think of a word like *cough*), and precede **i**. But **gh** can also be silent (*bough*, *high*) and replaced a middle English letter called *yogh* (!), strikingly similar when written to the number 3.

3 and 7 are holy numbers. 3 is half of eternity (8). Christ died when he was 33. Life began 3,000 million years ago. The sea covers 70% of the earth's surface. Its deepest part, the Mariana Trench, is 7 miles below sea level, where the pressure is 7 tons per square inch. Only 3% of water is fresh. A third of land is desert, etc. In phonetics, consonants are divided into 7 pairs of simple sounds. There are, however, another 7 consonantal sounds, which are complex. As a result, symbols are used in the International Phonetic Alphabet to represent them. These symbols, however, disguise their relation to the 7 pairs. They are, in fact, a combination of one of these and the letters **h/g**, as representing them in the following way reveals: **dh-th** (*brea<u>the</u>* - *brea<u>th</u>*), **gh-kh**

(*bridge* - *church*), **sh-zh** (*wish* - *vision*) and **ng** (*song*).

It is remarkable how many word connections are made by the addition of **h** or **g**. We have seen many examples: *love* makes us *whole*, Christ plants a *seed* in our *heart*, the *self* must go the way of all *flesh*, *fire* purifies in *grief*. The letter **h** engages with *I* to give *high*, it reminds us that *oil* is *holy*, it takes us away from *I'm* and points us to *him* or Christ.

Language appears desperate to get us away from the I. It is only a step from *me* to *we*. *Us* is the plural of *you*. The future auxiliary *will* combines with *I* to give *ill* (*I'll*), but with *we* it gives *well* (*we'll*)!

I would like to focus on three further connections made by the addition of **h**. This life and this world are a *gift*. We don't know where they come from. But it doesn't mean we have to *fight* over them because the author is temporarily absent. And yet this is what we do. We wish to control the flow of everything.

Here is a strange thing. There is food, shelter and warmth enough for everyone, every I, and yet because we control the flow of goods, because we lay claim to ownership and want money in return, *trade* produces a *dearth*. To *sell* produces *less*. It brings about *death* to the *earth*. The company is proud to blazon its name when selling the good, but is not much interested in the waste (which, however, still bears its name). The meaning of *market* is *cremate*, not *create*. The *economy* – politicians' top priority, which, we are led to believe, defines a nation's well-being – is the business of a few and could be renamed *Money & Co*. The reverse of *money* is *venom*. Language, I would suggest, is not in favour of a free market economy. Why should it be?

Time is money, we are told. Eternity is free. *Time* is a *myth*, a movable screen, connected with *die* (addition of **m**), *live* (**l-m**, **t-v**) and *I'm* (addition of **t**, **e**). It contains *I* and *me*. Time is a straight line teachers of English draw on a whiteboard, on which they mark the points past, present and future: stitches of time. We were born at some point in the past, we live now and will die at some point in the future. Time is countable and has to *begin* (connected with *being*) and *end*.

The line to be drawn needs the white space as a word needs a page and music needs silence. Silence stares at us through every word, not just before and after, but inside, around and even under every letter. This silence, or white space, is eternity and is here now. *Eternity*, like the whiteboard, contains *time* and is uncountable. We are in it now.

We go back to the image of the translator in no man's land, walking the narrow line like a tightrope walker with the balance of faith. At some point, we take our foot – eventually both feet – off the line and walk in thin air, with the balance of faith, like a tightrope walker or a spider spinning gossamer threads, only we mustn't look down or, like St Peter, we will sink.

Past, present and future. To mark these tenses, we make few changes to the verb, adding **s** in the third person singular of the present (*learn, learns*), which is also used to make nouns plural, **(e)d** or **t** in the past (*learned* or *learnt*) and sometimes **n** for the past participle (*know, known*). As we often add **h** and **g** to make word connections, so we often add one of these letters: **s, d-t, n**. Again we have seen frequent examples: *child/light - Christ, evil - devil, life - light, word - drown*. *Word* is the *sword* of angels: in icons, the sword (or Cross or spear) resembles a pen; *spear* is close to *speak* (**k-l-r**). We must *speak* in *peace*. We may only find *peace* when we *accept* a situation (as *refuse* is *suffer*). *Trip*, which has two meanings (journey and fall), is in *spirit*. *Search* contains *reach* as *seek* contains *see*.

The man was expelled from Eden and put to *work* in the *world* (**k-l**, addition of **d**). We cannot avoid working in this world, but if we *work*, if we have faith, we *grow* and receive the *crown* of salvation.

Other common additions are the letters **l** and **r**, which are used as suffixes in the English language to make adjectives and nouns. We have seen how *fire* and *life* are both in *rifle*! As we connected *sow* with *word*, we can connect *sow* with *soul* and *eros*. *Eros* is connected not only with *sore* and *rose* (the flower and past of *rise*), but also with *ore* and *roe*, *horse* and *shore*, even with *cross* and *cello*.

A very interesting connection by the addition of **r** is *I AM* with *Mary* (and *Mary* with *marry*). God – *I AM* in the Old Testament – chose the Virgin *Mary* to give birth to their Son. The two are linked.

The most common addition, however, is one we have already seen: the letter **e**, especially in final position. The reverse of *man* is *name*, of *no* is *one*. If we add **s**, *no* can be connected with *some*. *Fast* is in *feast* as *stay* is in *haste*, *waste* and *yeast*. *Rib* is in *bier* as *RIP* is in *ripe* and *pyre*. In the parable of the weeds of the field (Matthew 13.24-30, 36-43) – *parable* is *Braille*, a form of writing for the blind – we read that the devil sowed weeds among the wheat of the kingdom of heaven. *Weed* is connected with *wheat* by the pairs **a-e** and **d-t** (with addition of **h**). At the end of the age, when the time is *ripe*, Christ will send each *angel* to *glean* the field. Those committed of *rape* will *reap* their reward (Galatians 6.7: 'you reap whatever you sow'). Christ cries, 'Let anyone with ears to hear listen!' An ear is also of *wheat*, which is the meaning of true *wealth*.

Do stars have something to do with souls? A *star* seems to *stare*. It is like a *stair*. *Star* is connected with *past*, *start*, *rest* and *stir*. *Space* is *speak*, and both are in *escape*, as is *peace*.

We somehow have to focus our attention, concentrate our wills on a *single* point that is not ourselves, gather our *senses*. Then we will achieve *silence*. This happens in communal prayer. Another time I remember this happening was at the end of a performance of Shostakovich's Fourth Symphony by the Kirov Orchestra under Valery Gergiev in 2002. The conductor, who gets to control time, continued to hold his arms raised for a moment, pausing time, and there was absolute silence in the hall.

I do not trust any system based around the nation-state (lines drawn by humans). Real government goes on in the human heart, which is countable (beat) and uncountable (love). I do not trust anarchy because it says there is no leader. I do not trust democracy because it says power belongs to people. Democracy is built on choices. It allows us to express our differences.

I trust what Daniel Barenboim in his Reith Lectures describes, with reference to music, as 'hierarchy with equality.' We are all one body, and 'power belongs to God' (Psalm 62.11).

The conductor raises his arms *aloft* in another symbol of the Cross and begins to fly, to *float* in the sky.

. 7 .

This is how words are connected in the English language: by using the same letters (in the same order or rearranged), by changing the vowels, by changing the consonants (according to the phonetic pairs, the alphabet or their appearance) and by the addition of letters, most commonly **h, e, s, d-t, l-r, n** and **g**.

We have seen that Christianity contains paradoxes.

Having a veil over our eyes, we think that we see. Only when this veil is lifted do we realize that we are blind. When we draw a line through the I, we make the Cross, but we also make a plus-sign. In this way, we lose our life and find it at the same time.

Words that appear to be different, even opposites, turn out to be connected. *Starve*, connected with *breast*, is in *harvest* as *fast* is in *feast*. Examples we have seen are *bitter - sweet, light - dark/night, begin - end*. *No* is connected with *some* and, by the progression from A to I to O, with *an* and *any*. *Top* is in *bottom* (**b-p**, addition of **m**), *crown* is in *ground* (**g-k**, addition of **d**), *roof* is in *floor* (addition of **l**).

More opposites that turn out to be connected are *left - right* (**l-r, f-g**, addition of **h**), *north - south* (**r-s, n-u**), *east - west* (without the Greek letters alpha and omega), *local - global* (**b-c**, addition of **g**). Left and right, north and south, east and west are not so far apart; what happens locally affects us globally. We are *all one* (not *alone*!).

We find the same connection between words read back-to-front such as *be* and *ebb*. On the surface, they appear contradictory, like the ebb and flow of the sea or an expanding universe with receding galaxies or a dance such as the Procession of Echternach in which the pilgrim, to take three steps forward, takes two steps back. We must lose our life in order to find it. If we only lose it, we become stuck in the mud-flat of nostalgia. *Nostalgia* spells *lost again*. We remember people not where they were, but where they are now, and we pray for the dead. We remember past actions not to repeat them, but to repent. On the surface, *ebb* may appear to be an injustice, but then we discover that *die* without *l* contains *be*, even *die* and *live* are connected (**d-b-v**, addition of **l**).

Aer is in *water* and is the reverse of *sea*. A reflected landscape can look like the real thing, while the majority of air and sea creatures live close to (and frequently trespass) the dividing line, the sea's surface, remarkably similar viewed from below as it is from above.

We insist on ignoring the primal *law*, to love the *Lord* our God, and instead make of *law* its reverse: a *wall*. The law of God is to love him and to love our neighbour. The law of man is to protect his property, which he does by erecting walls (the absurdity of a wall is demonstrated by the need for a door to pass through it, which must then be locked, chained, bolted, alarmed, security cameras and lights fitted, guard dogs chained to stop them getting away, etc.).

It is often said that democracy and the rule of law represent freedom. Freedom, however, cannot be imposed, it is not a system. It comes from within, when we recognize that there is a God and submit ourself to him. It is a privileged moment in anyone's life when, in the stroke of an eye, God reveals himself. Our parameters change, we can no longer be the same, the borders of life and death are no longer valid because it is no longer only *this life*.

Democracy assumes the opposite. It applies only to this world and upholds the rights of the I to draw a line, say this is mine, I have a legal right to it and, if you want it, you must pay me. This encourages young people to study law and economics, which are professions of control, not service. The bills we pay in this life are not for the products we consume, but for the people who control them. Very little makes it into the fruit-picker's pocket; landlords very rarely build the house for which they charge rent. In this sense, democracy is true to its name, and power belongs to people.

Democracy insists on productivity, on noise, on activity. Noise has very little respect for the other and, worse, it prevents us from listening to the other. Only silence is reverential. Noise is democratic and, within legal boundaries, I have a right to make it. This productivity, or need to keep busy, is reflected in the language we speak. To make questions, negatives and tenses, we use what are called auxiliary verbs: *do* in the present (*Do you like? I don't like*), *have* in the past (*We have arrived*) and *will* in the future (*They will come*). These auxiliaries are strikingly reflective of our propensity to keep busy (*do*), to own or possess (*have*) and to want or desire (*will*). Only when we turn to the continuous aspect – to talk about something that is temporary (*I <u>was</u> living in Paris*), unfinished (*I <u>am</u> reading an interesting book*) or repeated (*I've <u>been</u> trying to find him*) – do we use the fourth auxiliary, *be*.

Democracy allows us to express our differences, and yet we all have the same needs. This *same* allows for *mass* production, keeping factory-lines moving. So this *differ* turns out to be a lie and is connected with *devil*.

It is the *Father* who would *gather* us into the fold. We recognize that we are one, we depend on God for everything, we give in (wonderful capitulation!) and, in return, receive the gift of eternal life. The limit of death turns out to be an illusion, a mere curtain. By passing through the eye of the needle, like rays of light through a jewel, by being bored by and in the end betraying our stubborn individuality and turning to God, we begin to make sense of this world, to have the wool pulled from our *eyes* so that we *see* (without *I*) that we are blind. We take two steps back in order to take three steps forward. The Cross becomes a plus-sign. The insect larva enters the pupa, its quiescent state, and emerges as a winged adult. We are in this *life* to learn how to *fly*. We turn *wall* into *walk*, and *door* into its reverse: *road*.

A reverse tells us something about the word. Like all word connections, it does not define a word, but frees it and gives it wings. To *live* is not to do *evil*. If we have *faith*, we must beware of the *thief* who would steal it. In fulfilment of the Old Testament (*new* is to *wean*), Christ says to Thomas, '*I am* the *way*.' The *truth hurts*, and yet without wings we are confined to the *lower world* (**d-e**). We cannot get off the ground. We are *heathen*, the reverse of which is *nether*. The reverse of *heaven* is *never*.

It is the job of the poet to see the similarity between different things, the job of the translator to heal the rift, to stitch time back into eternity, tirelessly criss-crossing the line like all those *diving birds* and *flying fish*. We use our *fin* as a *knife* to cut through the air and disappear behind time, until quite simply we are nowhere to be seen.

The reverse of *no* is *one*. If we make the progression from A to I to O, we turn *amen* into *mine* into *omen*, the reverse of which is *nemo*, the Latin for *no one*.

Perhaps the only *dogma* we can lay down with any confidence is its reverse: *am God*.

8

If God is *no one*, the translator is *no man*. He almost doesn't exist. His name is sometimes omitted. In commercial contracts, he receives 0.5% of the cover price of a paperback as royalties, which is set against the initial fee, so for every £10 the book is sold for, the translator receives 5p.

This is the lowly value we accord to translation, which

we consider second-rate, inferior, tainted. We prefer the original as we prefer the feel of a brand-new copy bought from a bookshop to that of a dog-eared copy borrowed from the library. And yet we are all translators, there is nothing we create. If we make something, we make it out of materials that already exist, we translate the clay. If we cook, we cook using the fruits, vegetables, meats, of the earth, which we translate. We open our mouths to feed, and translate (food into energy). We open our mouths to breathe, and translate (oxygen). We translate even in our mother's womb. We translate ideas that come to us. To translate is to give meaning, to name, as in Genesis 2.19 God brought every animal of the field and every bird of the air to Adam to name. This is our role: to carry across and, in the process, to find meaning.

When we start to translate, we may want to define the text, to explain it to ourselves. In this way, we limit the text, often introducing our own words, altering the meaning. To translate well, we must first understand the meaning so that, when it comes to the act of translation, we can remove the I and allow direct communication between the text and subsequent reader. We lose our life. This may sound self-destructive and impersonal. Far from it. The translation has passed through us at a given time, in a given frame of mind, and can never be repeated, with all its frailties and imperfections, as a conductor's interpretation of a piece of music, through his words, the musicians/their instruments, will never be the same. And if we do it well, meaning if we translate with love, *with the Holy Spirit*, as we hand over the text to the reader, we break away with meaning, greater understanding, greater knowledge. That is our part, and we are not the same.

We find this tendency to define in language. Look a word up in the dictionary, and you will find its definition. We have seen, however, that there is a whole dimension to words (read back-to-front, their consonants changed according to rules, etc.) that a dictionary does not list. A dictionary only gives us the horizontal, as if we only ever touched the surface of the sea (and never discovered its hidden depths, the amazing creatures with their psychedelic light shows that rise to the surface at night to feed).

In the beginning, God said, 'Let there be light,' and there was light. The I could never do this. A man can make a light, he is capable of containing it, harnessing it, it can come through him, but not from him. This is the difference between uncountable and countable nouns. Light is uncountable; a light is countable (there can be several of them). Abstract nouns like love, joy, pain, are generally uncountable. We experience them, we may be channels for them, but love is not mine. I prepare myself for love, I make room for love, I give and receive love. But I am not the author of love.

'God is love,' writes John in his first letter, and love, unlike my love, is inexhaustible. The terribly limited, man-made concept of capitalism relies precisely on the exhaustibility of products, their running out so that they have to be replaced, their countability. A line is drawn around them in a bottle, tin or packet, but what they contain continues for pint after pint and pound after pound. We limit ourselves to counting what comes in and what goes out, and taking a profit, so that what was once free becomes unaffordable or unavailable. And it is precisely the packaging – our definition – causing such a problem in the modern world.

It is not that we can do without definition. God himself counts the hairs on our head. It is that if we limit ourselves to definition, as with nostalgia, we only lose our life and do not find it. We draw a horizontal line, which represents a minus, a sum total or a stress, and fail to draw a vertical line, which, though it makes a Cross, also makes a plus. We fail to turn *define* into *divine*.

This tendency to define is found in other aspects of

language, for example the definite article and defining relative clauses. The definite article, *the*, is the most common word in the English language. Paul writes to the Ephesians about 'the unity of the faith and of the knowledge of the Son of God.' It is not just unity, but the unity of, it is not just faith or knowledge, but the faith and knowledge of, it is not just Son, but the Son of. It is, however, just God (unless we define him as 'the God of Israel'). Sadly people have other gods, they make God to be only countable, which he is not.

Defining relative clauses are clauses (subject and verb) introduced by a relative pronoun such as *who* or *that* without commas. The sentence *that I'm writing at the moment* contains a defining relative clause. Without it, the sentence does not make sense, unless I have referred to the sentence before. The sentence (I'm writing a sentence at the moment) contains a defining relative clause.

But I have a great love for non-defining relative clauses, which add extra information, and for the commas that surround them. My favourite example is found on a bridge in Kingston-upon-Thames, Surrey: 'Clattern Bridge, which crosses the Hogsmill River, is one of the oldest bridges in Surrey.' They don't have to be there, but they add something I wouldn't otherwise have known (that Clattern Bridge crosses the Hogsmill River). They give sudden verticality, depth.

Vertical contains *create* and *live*. We are vertical when we are alive, horizontal when we are dead. Death is the veil that enables us to live. Without it, we are just another line without fins or wings. Death gives balance to our life. We pass through the eye of the needle and discover that the translation we are working on already exists, which is why a translation in this life is always unfinished.

9

In this book, I have attempted to translate from the English language. When I started, I knew what I wanted to say, but along the way I have discovered new connections. The distinguished Greek poet Dimitris Allos describes poetry thus, as a way of learning, in which we receive and give back. Poetry, he says, is the language God uses to communicate, and we belong to the poem, not the poem to us. *Poem* in Old Church Slavonic means *we praise*.

This book is a communal song of praise to the Maker (which is the meaning in Greek of *poet*), who calls us to create – to translate – in his name. *God* in Greek is *theos*. We find him in the *other*. If we remove the final **s**, we find that God is *the O*. God the Father is O, God the Son O_2 and God the Holy Spirit O_3: three in ONE.

If we rotate the final E of ONE, we find that ONE gives us the letters O WN. These three letters – pronounced hŏ ōn and meaning *the Being, the One Who is*, in Greek – are found in the nimbus of icons of Christ, one letter in each of the shorter beams of the Cross. The longer beam is not visible, since Christ's body occludes it, but I suspect it might contain a dash, –, a horizontal I, which enables us to read the first four numbers, 0 to 3, anti-clockwise or by the sign of the Cross. We find these four numbers in a word such as WIND.

O WN spells three words in English: *own*, *won* and *now*. Christ claims us as his *own*. He has *won*. He is here *now*. If we imagine him as the Word, we speak him. If we imagine him as oxygen, we breathe him. If we imagine him with the Holy Spirit in water, we drink him. If we imagine him as the Sun, he lights our day

(DAY is found in A I O). And if we imagine him in the moon, he reflects his light at night.

In Slavonic countries, O WN is sometimes written O WH, H being N in Cyrillic, which rearranged spells *who* and *how*. In John 18.38, Pilate asks Jesus a fateful question, perhaps the most extraordinary question ever formulated by man: 'What is truth?' Jesus does not answer him, and that is because Pilate was standing in front of him without realizing that truth, like word, like love, like light, is a person. He didn't make the progression from A to I to O: from *what* to *why* to *who/how*. He should have asked, 'Who is truth?' and then Jesus might have replied, as he did to the Samaritan woman in John 4.26, to the man born blind in John 9.37, 'I am.'

The Tetragrammaton (which means *four letters*) is the Hebrew name of God in the Bible: YHWH. YHWH, which contains *why*, is related to the Hebrew verb (!) *hayah*, meaning *be*, and is composed entirely of breath and semi-vowels, no consonants. God is spiritual. God is the 'sound of sheer silence' Elijah heard on Mt Horeb in 1 Kings 19. 'Silence,' writes the Bulgarian poet Tsvetanka Elenkova in her foreword to my first book of poetry, 'is not the absence of sounds, but their harmony.'

Who is pronounced the same as the Sanskrit word

hu. We could read the name God tells to Moses in Exodus 3.14 not 'I AM WHO I AM,' but 'I AM HU I AM.'

Another name of God in the Old Testament is EL, which rotated gives us the numbers 73. Add 7 and 3, and you have 10, which again in reverse spells *no one*.

EL is *no one*. Christ is *who*: O WH. And here we have the second strong indication in language that Christ came to fulfil the prophets, because EL and O WH combine to make WHOLE. In numbers, they add up to 17, which gives 8, or eternity.

And so we make the progression from A to I to O: from *what* to *why* to *who*, from *draw* to *win* to *lose*, from *whale* to *while* to *whole* – a call from the depth of language – from *swan* to *swine* to *snow*.

If God expelled us from the garden of Eden, it wasn't a punishment. It was because we knew good and evil. We had made the progression from A to I and, had we then eaten of the tree of life, we would have remained there for ever, without knowing the other, as at Babel.

Who is love. 'I am,' says Jesus to Thomas. 'No I comes to the Father except through me.'

APPENDIX: SELECTED WORD CONNECTIONS

Some connections fit in more than one category. *Word - sow*, for example, can come under the alphabetical pair **r-s** and the addition of the letter **d**.

SAME LETTERS, SAME ORDER:

apart/a part
human/hu man
nowhere/now here

SAME LETTERS, DIFFERENT ORDER:

amen/mean, name
danger of need/garden of Eden
earth/heart
eros/rose, sore
evil/live, veil, vile
last/salt
listen/silent
lost again/nostalgia
miracle/reclaim

CHANGE OF VOWELS:

a-e
bread/breed
earth/three
faith/thief

a-o
road/door

a-u
start/trust

e-i
seed/dies

e-o
enemy/money

i-u
soil/soul

o-u
son/sun

CHANGE OF CONSONANTS – PHONETICS:

b-p
lamb/lamp
rib/RIP

d-t
child/light
word/water

f-v
define/divine
differ/devil

g-k
grow/work

l-r
heal/hear
law/war
life/fire
whole/whore

m-n
am/an
temper/repent

s-z
eros/zero

b-v-w-f
bread/water
breast/starve
breath/father
wall/fall

CHANGE OF CONSONANTS – ALPHABET:

a-b
air/bird
death/debt

b-c
believe/receive
birth/child
breath/create
global/local

d-e
God/ego
word/love
world/lower

f-g
father/gather
left/right

k-l
walk/wall
wicked/devil
work/world

l-m
land/man
line/mine
live/time

p-r
pain/rain
past/star

r-s
aer/sea
fear/safe
other/theos
word/sow

s-t
flesh/father

t-v
heathen/heaven
other/love

CHANGE OF CONSONANTS – APPEARANCE:

b-d
believe/veiled
birth/third
breath/thread

h-n
faith/faint
hope/open

i-l
body/blood
way/law

m-w
I am/way
me/we

n-r
know/work
pain/pray

n-u
anger/argue
north/south

v-y
devil/yield
venom/money

ADDITION OF LETTERS:

a
lst/last

b-v-w-f
earth, heart/breath, father
hole/whole

d-t
born/blind
hear/heart
I/die
see/seed

e
can/make
doubt/devout
fast/feast
first/strife
man/name
no/one
stay/yeast

g-k
fire/grief
see/seek

h
air/hair
dark/light
gift/fight
love/whole
one/home
self/flesh
water/father

i
be/die
green/energy
see/eyes

l-r
bosom/blossom
bud/blood
I am/Mary
sow/soul

m-n
create/cremate
day/dawn
sky/skin

s
child, light/Christ
reach/search
truth/thirst
word/sword

REVERSALS:

am God/dogma
and/DNA
be/ebb
heathen/nether
heaven/never
law/wall
less/sell

(A TO) I TO O:

am/I'm/om
amen/mine/omen
Christ/cross
draw/win/lose
live/love
nine/none
sin/son
what/why/who

JONATHAN DUNNE

was born in Kingston-upon-Thames, Surrey, in 1968 and educated at King's College School, Wimbledon. He studied Classics at Oxford University and lived in Spain for seven years, where he studied Spanish and Galician at Barcelona and Santiago de Compostela Universities. He now lives with his family in Bulgaria.

His first poetry collection, *Even Though That*, was published in 2004 with a parallel Bulgarian translation by Tsvetanka Elenkova and Rada Panchovska. His second book, *Alpha and Omega*, a collection of 24 Word poems, came out in 2007.

He translates from Bulgarian, Catalan, Galician and Spanish, including work by Tsvetanka Elenkova, Carme Riera, Manuel Rivas and Enrique Vila-Matas. His translations are published by Harvill Secker (Random House), New Directions and Overlook Press among others.

His poems have been published in Argentina, Bulgaria, Chile, England, Greece and Spain. His translations have appeared in *Absinthe*, *Modern Poetry in Translation*, *Poetry Wales* and the Shoestring Press anthology *Take Five 07*.

Jonathan Dunne can be contacted via the website www.smallstations.com.

ALSO FROM SMALL STATIONS PRESS:

Tsvetanka Elenkova,
TIME AND RELATION: Nine Essays about the Balkans etc.
(in Bulgarian)

For an up-to-date list of our publications, please visit our website:
www.smallstations.com